Dedication

This book is dedicated to my lovely husband, Zebulon Agocha. And my three beautiful children whom the Lord has graciously blessed me with, Angel, Heaven, and Ihichi. Thank you for being there and for believing in me when no one did.

****

To everyone who has developed strength by overcoming obstacles and fear, this book is for you.

special, indirect, incidental, or consequential damages, including, without limitation, lost revenues or lost profits, which may result from the use of the information contained in this book.

Foreword

From the first time I met Juliet 15 years ago, I knew she was going to be a star. She had all the qualities of a high-flying, glamorous leader with the most brilliant brain. She is one of the most intelligent people I have ever met. And she embodied a super-star image with class, charisma, and, most importantly, genuineness.

 Juliet exhibits humility, empowers others, stays authentic, and presents herself constantly and consistently. Today, as I write this foreword to her captivating book, "7 Ways To Overcome Fear", I share words that I always hoped—and in many ways knew—I would have the chance to write.

Preface

There is a prison with no physical key and no inmates but with millions of populations. It is a prison without walls but powerful, without barbed wire but can hold one in bondage, without guards and any physical barrier. But it is the most effective prison in the whole world. Few escape it and finds freedom. That prison is our mind. It is a prison that holds back our gifts, ministry, destiny, freedom, finances, and relationship, and, most importantly, it holds back the fulfillment of our full potential. But knowing that we can overcome fear and obstacles lays a solid foundation for success and teach us to become braver and more resilient.

"I sought the Lord, and He answered me and delivered me from all my fears. Those who look to Him are radiant, and their faces shall never be ashamed."

~ Psalm 34:4-5

"Look at the birds of the air; they do not sow, reap, or store away in barns, yet our heavenly Father feeds them. Are you not much more valuable than they? Worrying won't add a moment to your life. So, take your fears to the Lord; He will completely transform your life.

When God calls you for an assignment, it's often outside of your comfort zone. Do not be afraid; He is with you."

~ Juliet Agocha

7 WAYS TO
OVERCOME FEAR

By

Juliet Agocha

Contents

Overview

Fear is one of the most powerful emotions. It has a very strong effect on our mind and body. Thinking clearly and walking in your full glory is impossible when you're flooded with fear and obstacles. Overcoming obstacles and fears can be difficult but not impossible. The word "ob·sta·cle" is originally a Latin word that means something that stands, impedes, or hinders the way of progress. Obstacles can come in many forms, such as financial difficulties, relationship challenges, health issues, or personal insecurities. Obstacles can be difficult to overcome but can be conquered with the right mindset and support. In Hebrew words, fear means lack of courage, confidence, or someone who refuses to take meaningful action. So, if you put both definitions together, it simply means that obstacles impede us from taking significant action toward fulfilling our destiny. Fear is an emotional response to perceived danger or uncertainty that can limit our efforts and prevent us from pursuing our dreams. Fear is our most significant obstacle to happiness, freedom, and success! Obstacles impede our progress, and fear prevents us from pursuing our goals. Thus, limiting our personal growth and development, which negatively impact our self-esteem, confidence, and relationships. However, by understanding the root cause of these challenges, one can take steps to overcome them and live a more fulfilling life.

*"Our deepest fear is not that we are inade-
quate. Our deepest fear is that we are powerful beyond measure. We are beautiful,
unstoppable, extraordinary, and full of
light. Don't let fear dim your light.
Fear is a liar".*

~ Juliet Agocha

CHAPTER I

Introduction

Life is a journey full of challenges and uncertainties. Despite our best efforts, we all encounter obstacles that prevent us from reaching our goals and living our desired life. Fear is a natural and universal human emotion that we all experience at some point in our lives. Whether it's fear of failure, rejection, fear of the unknown, or change. These challenges can hold us back and limit our potential, whether financial difficulties, relationship issues, health problems, or personal insecurities.

However, the good news is that we can learn how to overcome our fears and live more courageous life. In this book, we will explore seven effective ways to overcome fear to take full control of our lives. These seven effective strategies are based on research, personal experiences, and practical exercises that will help you develop the skills and mindset needed to face your fears and move forward.

The purpose of this book is to provide practical and actionable advice, inspiration, and encouragement for overcoming obstacles and fear. Its goal is to empower individuals to take control of their lives, overcome challenges, and move forward with confidence, resilience, and purpose. Whether you're looking to improve your personal life, finances, relationships, or health, this booklet will provide valuable insights and guidance to help you achieve your goals.

Fear Is Our Biggest Obstacle

Fear is a powerful and natural emotion that is part of the human experience. It can help us stay safe in dangerous situations, but it can also hold us back and limit our potential. When fear becomes a constant presence in our lives, it can prevent us from taking risks, pursuing our goals, and living the life we truly desire. In many ways, fear is our biggest obstacle.

Fear is often rooted in our past experiences and can be triggered by anything that reminds us of those experiences. This can lead to irrational and overwhelming feelings that make it difficult to move forward. For example, someone who experienced a traumatic event in the past may become anxious and avoidant in situations that remind them of that event. This type of fear can be so strong that it affects daily life and prevents one from pursuing new opportunities.

However, our thoughts and beliefs can also imagine and create fear. We may fear failure, rejection, or the unknown, even if there is no concrete evidence to support those fears. This type of fear can be particularly challenging because it is often based on our negative self-talk and limiting beliefs.

The impact of fear on our personal and professional growth cannot be overstated. When we allow fear to control our actions and decisions, we miss valuable opportunities for growth and learning. We may stay in a job or relationship that no longer serves us, avoid trying new things or limit ourselves in other ways. This can lead to a sense of stagnation and unfulfillment.

Overcoming fear is not only crucial for your personal and developmental growth but also important for your spiritual growth. It helps individuals break free from limiting thoughts and beliefs, take action toward their goals, and live a more gratifying life. Individuals can build resilience and develop a positive outlook on life by overcoming challenges. This can help improve self-esteem, confidence, and relationships, leading to a cycle of positive thoughts and contentment. Moreover, overcoming obstacles and fear can help individuals pursue their passions and reach their full potential. Whether it's starting a new business, seeking a new career, giving love a second chance, or simply living life to the fullest, overcoming these challenges is essential for personal growth and success. Life does not get easier as we get older. Instead, it demands more on our lives, finances, emotions, and time. Overcoming fear and what is stopping you from taking the next step forward to achieving your dream is essential for personal growth. Recognize that every situation you find yourself in is not there to destroy you but to inspire your continued growth.

"Fear is only as deep as the mind allows."

~ Japanese Proverb

CHAPTER II

Defining Obstacles
and Fear

To better understand how fear can become our biggest obstacle, it's essential to define what obstacles and fear are.

Obstacles and fear are two powerful forces that can shape an individual's life and limit their potential.

At their core, obstacles are any hindrance or challenge that stands in the way of personal growth and success. Obstacles are challenges that we face in life that can prevent us from achieving our goals and living the life we desire. Obstacles can take many forms, such as financial difficulties, relationship challenges, health problems, and personal insecurities. These challenges can be rooted in negative thoughts, beliefs, and past experiences, making them difficult to overcome. The key is that obstacles are perceived as challenges or barriers we must overcome to achieve our desired outcomes.

At the same time, fear is an emotional response to perceived danger or uncertainty that limits one's actions and prevents individuals from taking risks. It can manifest in various ways, including anxiety, panic, and avoidance behaviors. Fear can also come in many forms, including fear of failure, fear of rejection, fear of the unknown, and fear of change.

When fear becomes an obstacle, it can manifest in various ways. It can prevent us from taking risks or pursuing opportunities, keep us in our comfort zone, or create self-doubt and limiting beliefs. Fear can also cause us to engage in negative self-talk or engage in unhelpful behaviors, such as procrastination or avoidance.

How Fear works

Fear is a natural and essential human emotion that is designed to protect us from perceived danger or harm. The experience of fear involves a complex interplay of cognitive, emotional, and physiological responses that prepare us to respond to potential threats.

When we encounter a perceived threat or danger, our brains activate the amygdala, which is the brain's alarm system that signals the release of stress hormones such as adrenaline and cortisol. These hormones trigger a cascade of physiological responses that prepare the body for action, such as an increased heart rate, rapid breathing, and heightened alertness. This physiological response is known as the "fight or flight" response, which helps us confront or escape the perceived threat.

At the same time, our brains also engage in a cognitive and emotional process of evaluating the threat and determining the appropriate response. This process involves the prefrontal cortex, which is responsible for decision-making and risk assessment, and the limbic system, which is responsible for regulating emotions. Together, these brain regions process information about the threat and determine the appropriate action.

Various factors, such as past experiences, learned associations, culture, and social influences, can influence our experiences of fear. For example, an individual may develop a fear of dogs due to a past negative experience with a dog, or they may learn to associate dogs with danger due to cultural beliefs or social messaging.

While fear is a natural and essential emotion, excessive or irrational fears can lead to significant distress and impairment in daily life. Anxiety disorders, such as phobias and panic disorder, are characterized by extreme and persistent fear responses that interfere with daily functioning. Effective treatments for these disorders include cognitive-behavioral therapy, exposure therapy, and medication, which can help individuals learn to manage their fears and develop more adaptive responses to perceived threats.

Understanding The Symptoms of Fear

Experiencing occasional fear and anxiety is a normal part of life. However, people with persistent fear about everyday situations involve repeated episodes of sudden feelings of intense anxiety and fear that reach a peak within minutes. Common obstacles and fear signs and symptoms include:

Financial obstacles are common obstacles that individuals face, as they can limit their ability to reach their goals and live the desired life. For example, mortgage or car payments can eat up extra monthly income. If you've recently upgraded your car or just bought a new house, you might feel like you're always making payments but never paying them off. When your expenses exceed your income, it creates fear in you. The first step to overcoming this obstacle is to set a monthly budget and stick to it.

Relationship Obstacles are another common obstacle that individuals face, as they can impact one's self-esteem, confidence, and personal life. While the last thing partners want to think about is breaking up, the sad reality is that it happens—a lot, and many don't see a breakup coming. Additionally, infidelity is increasingly becoming one of the most common relationship challenges in romantic relationships. Individuals who are facing relationship difficulties may feel limited in their ability to form meaningful connections with others and pursue their goals.

Health Obstacles can also limit personal growth and development, impacting an individual's physical and emotional well-being. For example, individuals who are dealing with chronic health issues may feel limited in their ability to pursue their passions and reach their full potential. Many people wish to create a clear vision or improve their health but need help because adopting new habits is relatively difficult.

Personal insecurities can keep individuals from pursuing their passions and reaching their goals. Your beliefs about yourself and your word are crucial to overcoming insecurities. If you believe you are shy, worthless, vulnerable, and not deserving of success, your actions will follow this limiting belief pattern.

Types of Fears

Phobias

A phobia is a type of fear that is characterized by intense and persistent fear or anxiety related to a specific object, situation, or activity. Fear is often excessive and unreasonable, leading to significant distress and avoidance behaviors.

To recognize a phobia, you may observe that the person experiences intense and persistent fear or anxiety when exposed to the object or situation or when anticipating the encounter with the object or situation.

The fear or anxiety is often accompanied by physical symptoms such as sweating, trembling, rapid heartbeat, and difficulty breathing.

People with phobias often go to great lengths to avoid the object or situation that triggers their fear, which can significantly impact their daily life and functioning.

Social anxiety

Social anxiety, also known as social anxiety disorder, is a type of fear characterized by an intense and persistent fear of social situations or performance situations in which the individual may feel judged, evaluated, or scrutinized by others.

People with social anxiety disorder experience significant fear or anxiety about embarrassment, humiliation, or rejection in social situations, such as speaking in public, meeting new people, eating in front of others, or participating in group activities. Social anxiety is a type of fear because it is a natural response to a perceived threat or danger. In social situations, the threat may be a perceived negative evaluation by others, which triggers the fear response.

Agoraphobia

Agoraphobia is a type of fear that is characterized by an intense and persistent fear of situations in which escape may be intricate, or help may not be available in case of a panic attack or other perceived danger. This fear can lead to avoidance behaviors that can significantly impact the person's daily life and functioning.

Agoraphobia can involve a fear of a wide range of situations, such as crowded public places, open spaces, public transportation, or being alone outside the home.

Existential fears

Existential fears are a type of fear that is related to one's existence, meaning, and purpose in life. These fears can arise from a sense of uncertainty or lack of control over the future or from an awareness of mortality and the impermanence of life.

Examples of existential fears may include fear of death, fear of the unknown, fear of meaninglessness, isolation, and fear of the future. These fears can lead to anxiety, depression, and a sense of disconnection from others and the world.

Fear of failure is a common fear that individuals face. Many of us are afraid of failing even before we try. Fear of failure (also known as "atychiphobia") is when we allow that fear to stop us from doing the things that can move us forward to achieve our goals. Different things, such as negative feelings into adulthood or experiencing a traumatic event in life, low self-esteem, or anxiety, can cause this.

Fear of rejection is another common fear that individuals face. This can be in business, academics, relationships, or social media. Fear of rejection can cost people a great deal in their careers or personal life, including missing out on good opportunities and business investments, not asking for pay increases, or staying stuck in their current position due to fear of rejection.

Fear of the unknown is a feeling of uncertainty that can bring acute discomfort. For some people, a general inability to process ambiguous situations can fuel chronic anxiety disorders. This can hold individuals back from trying new things and pursuing their passions.

WHY DOES UNCERTAINTY MAKE US SO UNEASY?

Image credit: iStock

We can't alleviate all the life chal-lenges that come our way, and we wouldn't want to even if we could.

Some trials and tribulations are natural and necessary for our growth; it gives us zing of energy to get things done—the spice results from the hormone flooding the system when the body detects danger or fear. Uncertainty is part of life, and we cannot avoid it. But it's perceived as unsafe and potentially painful. Whether the situation is positive or negative, our brain prefers something familiar to something unfamiliar. When most of us think of fear, we become uneasy. But in reality, uncertainty helps us to learn how to overcome fear by liberating the pursuits we can undertake.

Why Identifying Fears is important

Photo credit: Istock

Identifying your fears is essential to personal growth, self-awareness, and mental health. Here are some of the key reasons why it is necessary to identify your concerns:

Improve self-awareness

Identifying your fears can help you better understand your thoughts, emotions, and behaviors. This increased self-awareness can help you recognize patterns in your thinking and understand how your fears may impact your daily life.

Build resilience

Facing your fears can be a challenging and uncomfortable experience, but it can also help you to build resilience and develop coping strategies. When you confront your fears, you learn that you are capable of handling difficult situations and that you can overcome obstacles.

Increase confidence

Overcoming your fears can also increase your confidence and self-esteem. You feel a sense of accomplishment and pride when you face your fears and come out to the other side. This can help you to build a positive self-image and to feel more confident in your abilities.

Enhance personal growth

Identifying and overcoming your fears can be a powerful catalyst for personal growth and development. When you confront your fears, you may discover new strengths, skills, and interests that you didn't know you had. This can open up new opportunities for personal and professional growth.

Improve mental health

Fear and anxiety can significantly contribute to mental health issues such as depression and anxiety disorders. By identifying your fears, you can begin to address the underlying causes of your anxiety and take steps to manage it more effectively. This can lead to improved mental health and overall well-being.

How to Identify Your Fears

Fear arises out of a specific part of the brain, and it allows emotion to overcome rational thought. Something triggers fear in the form of anxiety. When you start experiencing anxiety over something, know that fear is coming forth. Try to distract yourself with a different thought by using the other part of your brain. Think about pictures, parties, vacations, family, or good memories. For example, stop and analyze a distant memory. Try using an image to remember an old friend or a good restaurant.

Write in a journal

Writing in a journal can help you to explore your thoughts and emotions more intensely. You can identify patterns and themes by recording your fears and the situations that trigger them. Learning to overcome fear is much like any problem-solving challenge; you must identify the challenge to overcome it. What is it you're afraid of? Going back to school, your ministry, business, family, job, career, relationship, or personal goals. Sit quietly for a few minutes and observe your thoughts and feelings. Write down what comes up, and be as specific as you can.

Ask for feedback

Sometimes, others can see things in us that we cannot see ourselves. Ask trusted friends, family members, or colleagues if they have noticed any patterns in your behavior that might indicate underlying fears.

Use visualization techniques

Visualization techniques involve imagining a scenario in which you confront and overcome your fears. This can help you to identify what it is that you are specifically afraid of, as well as provide a roadmap for overcoming those fears.

Practice mindfulness

Mindfulness involves being present at the moment and observing your thoughts and emotions without judgment. By practicing mindfulness, you can become more aware of the ideas and ecofeminists driving your fears. Consider embracing a daily 5-10 minutes mindfulness meditation to gain profound clarity on what drives you. Relax and begin to imagine yourself handling the situation peacefully. As you find your center, you'll feel empowered to confront your fears.

"The brave man is not he who does not feel afraid, but he who conquers that fear."

~ Nelson Mandela.

CHAPTER III

7 Ways to Overcome Fear

You have done the hard work by identifying your fear. Now, it's time to conquer your fear and use it to your advantage. Here are Seven powerful ways to overcome fear and obstacles so you can live life to its fullest

Adopt A Growth Mindset

No one is ever perfect, so stop striving for that. Perfection only exists on social media, not in real life. People often show the good side of their journey and not the struggling part. Everyone wants to paint a "perfect" picture to the public so they don't look mediocre. With a growth mindset, you are more likely to be resilient in the face of obstacles. Take risks, and see challenges as opportunities for growth and development. Believe you can make progress one day at a time and that you're capable of it – the fear will lose you bold.

Daily Affirmations

Daily positive affirmations are powerful tools that individuals can use to overcome fear. Visualizing success can help individuals stay motivated and focused, and affirmations can help build self-confidence and reduce negative self-talk. When visualizing, imagine yourself successfully overcoming your obstacle and focusing on the positive emotions that come with it. Affirmations are positive statements that individuals can repeat to themselves to build confidence and reduce self-doubt. For example, instead of saying, "I'm not good enough," try saying, "I am capable and confident in my abilities." "I am good enough." "I deserve joy."

Show Gratitude and Mindfulness

Gratitude and mindfulness can play a role in cultivating a positive attitude toward fear. Focus on the positives in life, even when faced with challenges. Discuss how mindfulness can help individuals stay present and focused, reducing feelings of stress and anxiety. Shift negative self-talk to more positive and constructive thoughts. For example, Be thankful to the person who cooked for you. Be grateful for your good health. Be thankful for the one good friend who calls or texts to check on you.

Face Your Fear Head-On

The first step in overcoming fear is to confront it head-on. This means actively seeking out situations that make you uncomfortable and pushing yourself to face them. By doing this, you can develop a sense of mastery and control over your fear and build confidence in your ability to handle difficult situations.

Embrace Positive Self-Talk

Positive self-talk is a powerful tool for overcoming fear. Engaging in positive self-talk reinforces our confidence and reminds us of our strengths and abilities. This helps us approach difficult situations with a positive attitude and reduces fear's power over us.

Celebrate Your Victories

Celebrating your victories, no matter how small they may be, is important. Get a nice long therapeutic massage, get your nails done, watch a good Netflix movie, go to a nice restaurant and treat yourself, take a day off to pamper yourself, or take care of those sores you may have ignored to get things done. Recognizing and celebrating your achievements reinforces your confidence and builds momentum toward overcoming future obstacles.

Accept That You'll Fail

Everyone fails. Celebrities, entrepreneurs, world leaders, pastors, CEOs. Business owners, engineers, and doctors. The issue is that our society shies away from talking about failure. Everybody wants to package success and sell it, creating the false impression that to be truly success-ful, you must always succeed. Many people live fake lives on social me-dia, so never compare your real life to a filtered lifestyle. Part of over-coming fear is recognizing that you'll fail because everyone on the planet – including those you know, love, and admire – has encountered failures on their path to greatness. How you respond to fear sets you apart from the rest of the crowd. - Jack Canfield. (n.d.). "Everything you want is on the other side of fear."

The Impact of Fear and Obstacles on Our Life

Fear can profoundly impact our life, affecting personal growth and development, self-esteem, confidence, and relationships. These challenges can limit individuals from pursuing their passions, reaching their goals, and living fulfilling lives. Moreover, obstacles and fear can be rooted in negative thoughts, beliefs, and past experiences, making them difficult to overcome.

The impact of obstacles and fear can manifest in different ways, including decreased self-esteem, limited personal growth and development, negative thoughts, and decreased confidence. These challenges can also affect personal relationships and limit one's ability to form meaningful connections with others. Fear can also prevent individuals from taking risks, pursuing their goals, and exploring new opportunities, leading to frustration, disappointment, and regret. A positive mindset and attitude towards obstacles can significantly determine how individuals perceive and handle challenges.

A growth mindset, where individuals view obstacles as opportunities for growth and development, is more likely to result in success and satisfaction compared to a fixed mindset, where individuals believe their abilities and traits are fixed and cannot be changed. A positive attitude towards obstacles means accepting that challenges are normal and viewing them as opportunities for growth and development. This mindset enables individuals to approach barriers with a sense of curiosity, determination, and optimism, which can help them overcome challenges and achieve their goals. In contrast, a negative attitude towards obstacles can lead to frustration, hopelessness, and defeat. This type of mindset can prevent individuals from taking action, trying new things, and pursuing their goals. It's essential to cultivate a positive attitude towards obstacles by focusing on the benefits of facing challenges and developing a growth mindset. By doing so, individuals will be better equipped to handle obstacles and overcome fear, leading to gradational success and fulfillment.

"Fear is not real. The only place where fear can exist is our thoughts of the future. It is a product of our imagination, causing us to fear things that are not at present and may never exist."

~ Will Smith.

CHAPTER IV

Challenge your thoughts

Photo Credit: Fotolia

Explanation of how thoughts can contribute to fear

Our thoughts can significantly contribute to our experience of fear. Fear is a natural and adaptive emotion that helps us respond to real or perceived threats. Still, sometimes our thoughts can exaggerate or distort the actual danger, leading to excessive or irrational fear.

For example, imagine you are walking alone at night, and you hear a strange noise. You might immediately think it is a dangerous person or animal, and your body may respond with a surge of fear. However, something harmless may have caused the noise, like a fallen branch or a stray cat. In this case, your thoughts contributed to your experience of fear, even though the actual danger was minimal.

Techniques For Challenging Negative Thoughts

Identify the negative thought.

Pay attention to your thoughts when you feel afraid, and try to identify the negative thought that is contributing to your fear. For example, you might be thinking, "I'm going to die," "I'm not safe," or "I can't handle this."

Evaluate the thought

Once you have identified the negative thought, evaluate it objectively.

Ask yourself if it is based on facts or assumptions, and whether it is realistic or exaggerated. For example, you might ask, "Is it really true that I'm going to die?" or "What evidence do I have that I'm not safe?"

Challenge the thought

After evaluating the negative thought, challenge it by finding evidence that contradicts it. For example, you might remind yourself of times when you have felt safe in similar situations or recall statistics showing low danger. You can also reframe the thought in a more positive and realistic way. For example, instead of thinking, "I can't handle this," you could think, "I can handle this by taking small steps and seeking help if I need it."

Repeat the positive thought

Once you have challenged the negative thought and replaced it with a more positive and realistic one, repeat the positive thought to yourself several times. This can help reinforce the new thought and reduce your fear.

CHAPTER V

Seeking Inspiration from Others

We all face obstacles and fears in our lives, and overcoming them on our own can be challenging. Fortunately, seeking inspiration from others can provide us with the encouragement and motivation we not take action and ress. In this chapter, we will explore the benefits of seeking inspiration from others and the various ways in which we can do so.

Benefits of Seeking Inspiration from Others

It provides a new perspective

Hearing the stories and experiences of others can help us to gain a new perspective on our own challenges and fears.

Offers encouragement

Knowing that others have faced similar obstacles and overcome them can be incredibly encouraging and give us the confidence to keep going.

Increases motivation

Seeing others succeed can increase our motivation to pursue our goals and overcome our fears.

Enhances our support network

Building relationships with others who share similar goals and struggles can provide us with a supportive network of like-minded individuals who can encourage and motivate us.

Ways to Seek Inspiration from Others

Attend motivational speeches or events: Attending motivational speeches or events can be a great way to hear from inspiring individuals and gain new perspectives.

Read biographies and memoirs

Reading about the lives and experiences of successful individuals can inspire us and encourage us to pursue our own goals.

Seek out role models

Identifying individuals who embody the qualities and characteristics we admire can be a powerful source of inspiration.

Participate in support groups or workshops

Joining a support group or workshop focused on overcoming obstacles and fears can provide us with a supportive community of individuals who can inspire and encourage us.

Connect with others online

Joining online forums, groups, or social media communities focused on overcoming obstacles and fears can provide us with a virtual support network and access to inspiring stories and experiences.

Seeking inspiration from others can be a powerful tool in overcoming our obstacles and fears. Whether it's through attending motivational speeches, reading biographies, seeking out role models, or connecting with others online, the support and encouragement we receive can help us take action and progress towards our goals. So let's start seeking inspiration from others and find the encouragement we need to overcome our obstacles and fear and reach new heights of success.

"He who is not every day conquering some fear has not learned the secret of life."

~ Ralph Waldo Emerson

CHAPTER VI

Encouragement and Action

Taking action is a crucial step in overcoming fear. Fear can cause us to feel powerless and helpless, which can prevent us from taking the necessary steps to overcome it. By taking action, we can break through our fear and gain a sense of control and empowerment.

When we take action, we demonstrate to ourselves that we can progress and achieve our goals. This can lead to increased confidence and self-efficacy, which can, in turn help us overcome future fears. Taking action can also allow us to identify the specific steps we need to take to overcome our fear and achieve our goals.

The importance of taking action

One of the biggest obstacles to overcoming fear is inaction. People often become overwhelmed by the thought of change and the fear of the unknown, and they may become paralyzed as a result. However, it's essential to understand that taking action is the key to overcoming obstacles and fear. Whether it's by facing fear head-on, starting to work on a project, or seeking help from others, taking action is the way to start making progress. By taking the first step, you'll begin to see the results of your efforts and build momentum toward a brighter future.

Techniques for taking action

Set small goals

Setting small, achievable goals can help you make progress toward your larger goal. For example, if you fear public speaking, you could start by giving a presentation to a small group of friends or family members. As you become more comfortable, you can gradually increase the size of your audience.

Break tasks into manageable steps

Breaking a task into smaller, more manageable steps can make it feel less daunting and easier to tackle. For example, if you fear flying, you could break the task into smaller steps, such as researching flights, booking a flight, packing for the trip, and arriving at the airport.

Use exposure therapy

Exposure therapy is a technique that involves gradually exposing yourself to the thing you fear in a controlled and safe environment. For example, if you have a fear of heights, you could start by looking at pictures of heights and then progress to standing on a low platform and gradually working your way up to higher platforms.

Use relaxation techniques

Fear can cause physical symptoms such as sweating, shaking, and increased heart rate. Relaxation techniques such as deep breathing, meditation, and visualization can help reduce these symptoms and make it easier to take action.

Get support

Having the support of friends, family, or a therapist can make it easier to take action and overcome fear. Support can provide encouragement, accountability, and a safe space to talk about your fears and progress.

By using these techniques for taking action, you can gradually overcome your fear and achieve your goals. Remember, taking action doesn't have to be a big, dramatic step - even small steps can make a big difference over time.

Encouragement to take small steps

It's important to remember that over-coming obstacles and fear is a journey, not a destination. You don't have to do everything all at once. Instead, focus on taking small, manageable steps. It could be as simple as setting a goal for the day or week or taking a small action that moves you closer to your goal. Whatever it is, focus on making progress, no matter how small. Over time, these small steps will add up, and you'll find yourself making substantial progress toward overcoming your obstacles and fears.

Taking action can have a powerful impact on our confidence and sense of control. When we take action, we demonstrate to ourselves that we can progress and achieve our goals. This can increase our self-efficacy and belief in our ability to overcome future challenges.

For example, if we fear public speaking, taking action might involve joining a public speaking group and practicing in front of a supportive audience. By taking action in this way, we can improve our skills and confidence and reduce our fear of speaking in front of others.

Similarly, if we have a fear of flying, taking action might involve gradually exposing ourselves to the experience of flying, starting with shorter flights and progressively increasing the length and complexity of the journey. By taking action in this way, we can gradually reduce our fear of flying and increase our confidence in our ability to handle the experience.

How Overcoming Fear Can Positively Impact Our Life

Overcoming obstacles and fear can have a profound impact on one's life. by facing your fears and working to overcome your obstacles, you'll gain confidence, self-esteem, and a greater sense of control over your life. you'll also develop new skills, build stronger relationships, and open up new opportunities for growth and success. by taking control of your life and facing your fears, you'll begin to experience a greater sense of purpose and fulfillment, and you'll be able to live the life you've always wanted.

Image by deposit

"Obstacles are like wild animals. They are cowards, but they will bluff you if they can. If they see you are afraid of them... they are liable to spring upon you, but if you look them squarely in the eye, they will slink out of sight."

Orison Swett Marden (n.d.).

CHAPTER VII

Inspiring Stories of People Who Have Overcome Fear

Story of Sarah,

The cancer survivor turned marathon runner

Sarah was diagnosed with stage 4 cancer at the age of 25. Despite the odds against her, she fought through numerous rounds of chemotherapy and radiation therapy. During her treatment, Sarah became interested in running and started jogging around the block. With each passing day, she increased her distance and before long, she was running marathons. In less than two years after her diagnosis, Sarah ran her first marathon and finished at 4 hours and 30 minutes.

Story of Jack,

The small business owner

Jack was a recent college graduate with an excellent idea for a business, but he needed more money to start it. Instead of giving up, he found alternative ways to fund his business, such as crowdfunding and working part-time. Despite many obstacles and setbacks, Jack's determination and hard work paid off, and his business quickly grew. Today, Jack is the owner of a successful small business, and he's proud to have overcome the challenges he faced to get there.

Story of Emily,

The artist with a physical disability

Emily was born with a physical disability that limited her movement and ability to create art in the traditional sense. However, she didn't let that stop her from pursuing her passion. Emily taught herself to paint with her mouth, and her unique style soon gained recognition. Today, Emily is an accomplished artist with her work displayed in galleries around the world, and she's an inspiration to others who may face similar challenges.

Story of David,

The Business Leader with a Difficult Childhood

David grew up in a disadvantaged household and faced many challenges in his childhood. Despite these challenges, David was determined to succeed, and he worked hard to get a good education and build a successful career. Today, David is a well-respected business leader, and he uses his success to give back to his community and help others who may be facing similar challenges.

These stories show that anyone can overcome their obstacles and reach their full potential, no matter what challenges they face. Whether you're facing a personal challenge, a professional obstacle, or a difficult situation in your life, these stories provide inspiration and motivation to help you overcome your own obstacles and reach your full potential.

CHAPTER VIII

Conclusion

In this booklet, we have delved into the world of obstacles and fear and the impact they can have on our lives. We have defined what obstacles and fear are, and explored the common experiences that people face. Furthermore, we have covered a variety of ways to overcome these challenges, including developing a positive mindset and attitude, practical solutions and techniques, personal anecdotes and experiences, inspiring stories, and encouragement to take action. The key points covered in this booklet are crucial to understanding the nature of obstacles and fear and the various ways in which they can be overcome. These points include Understanding what obstacles and fear are and the common experiences that people face. The importance of developing a positive mindset and attitude towards obstacles. Practical solutions and techniques for overcoming obstacles and fear. Inspiring stories and personal experiences of overcoming challenges. Encouragement and action towards taking small steps. The positive impact of overcoming obstacles and fear n one's life. One of the central themes of this booklet is the importance of a positive mindset and attitude when facing obstacles and fear. This means approaching these challenges with determination, resilience, and a willingness to learn and grow. By developing this type of mindset, you can overcome any obstacle and fear that may come your way. In addition to a positive mindset, some practical solutions and techniques can be used to overcome obstacles and fear. These can include things like setting achievable goals, using positive affirmations, seeking support from others, and practicing sself-care Each of these techniques has the potential to help you over-come the challenges you face and build the confidence you need to keep moving forward. Personal an-ecdotes and experiences can also play a significant role in overcoming obstacles and fear. You can gain hope and inspiration by learning from others who have faced similar challenges and overcome them. This can help you to see that it is possible to overcome the obstacles and fear that you may be facing and that you are not alone in your journey. The inspiring stories of people who have overcome obstacles and fear can be potent. These stories can serve as a reminder that even the most significant challenges can be overcome with determination, hard work, and a positive attitude. By learning from these stories, you can gain new insights, a greater understanding of your obstacles, and be inspired to take action to overcome them.

In conclusion, you have been provided with an overview of the obstacles and fear that people face and seven powerful ways in which they can be overcome. It is important to remember that change takes time and effort. Taking small steps toward overcoming obstacles and fear can lead to significant results. It is crucial to approach these challenges with a positive attitude and determination. By doing so, you can overcome any obstacle and fear that may come your way and live a fulfilling and successful life.

Acknowledgments

Writing a book is harder than I thought and more rewarding than I could ever imagine. None of this would have been possible without GOD ALMIGHTY. I thank GOD for bestowing me with His infinite wisdom, creativity, and abundant life. I want to express my deep gratitude to my husband, children, and my entire family. I am incredibly thankful to my mother, Irene Ike, for keeping up with my children while I disappeared to my home office—a massive shoutout to my father, Sylvester Ike Ndukwu (RIP), for believing in me. I thank friends and loved ones who have encouraged and inspired me throughout this journey. Your kindness and encouragement have helped me to stay focused.

Also, I extend my thanks to those who have shared their personal experiences and insights with me, providing me with a deeper understanding of the challenges and triumphs of overcoming obstacles and fear. Your stories have touched my heart and will no doubt inspire others as they read this book.

About the Author

Juliet is a well-established name and has contributed extensively to the world of leadership. She is internationally recognized and celebrated for her immersing work, especially in the Technology industry. She is the CEO of **ULTIMATE**

WEB DESIGN, a technology company that creates affordable, high-performance websites for small business owners.

Juliet completed her Bachelor's degree in Information Technology from Columbia Southern University, Alabama, USA. And her master's degree in Cybersecurity with honors from American Public University, West Virginia, U.S.A. With several industrial certifications hanging on her wall, Juliet is a lifelong learner who is currently completing her Ph.D. program in Leadership with the University of the Cumberlands, with a second master's degree in MBA.

In addition to being a prolific author, Juliet is a devoted philanthropist. Her most significant efforts are dedicated to preaching the gospel of Jesus Christ as a motivational speaker and helping men and women to overcome their daily challenges.